Amazing Amusing Emus

Yesterday's Dinosaurs On Today's Farm

Amazing Amusing Emus

Yesterday's Dinosaurs On Today's Farm

by Elizabeth Thwing

Kireli Press

2014

First Printing: 2014

ISBN-13: 978-1500407001

ISBN-10:1500407003

Photographs by Elizabeth and Kirby Thwing unless otherwise credited.

Kireli Publications
15 Pond Road
Hawley, MA 01339

Website—https://sites.google.com/site/amazingamusingemus

DEDICATION

A very special thank you to my husband "Lark" for his unfailing support of me and this book. Without his technical expertise, *Amazing Amusing Emus* would have remained a pipe dream.

Table of Contents

Words with an asterisk (*) appear in the glossary.

ACKNOWLEDGMENTS

It required a knowledgeable contingent of folks to give birth to this book, and I owe a debt of gratitude to all of the following people. First, my many thanks and sincere appreciation to Stanley and Geri Johnson and Dee Dee Mares of Songline Emu Farm, for without them and their invaluable support, there would be no emu book! I thank Maria Minnaar, co-author/illustrator of the *Emu Farmer's Handbook* and author/illustrator of the *Emu Farmer's Handbook, Volume II*, for her generosity in allowing me to use two illustrations from her books. Also Patrick Getty, who as adjunct paleontologist to the Springfield Science Museum, validated my historical information. A huge thank you to Pam Shrimpton, who copy-edited the book, and to Doogie Horner for designing its elegant cover. My thanks to the multiple readers of this manuscript, including author Stephen Swinburne. To Joylene Reavis, Myra Charleston and Betty Lou Cauffman of the American Emu Association for answering all my questions and providing more information and photos than I asked for. To Deborah Vetter from the Institute of Children's Literature for imparting writing knowledge, her moral support and professional expertise. To Dan Augustino, Joanna Hanna and Richard Anderson of the Springfield Museums, Springfield, MA for answering more questions and for providing important tips and information. To Lara Kirkendall of the Sacramento Zoo and Lisa Land of the Cougar Mountain Zoo. To Armand Morgan, Yale University Peabody Museum of Natural Sciences educator, for his time at the very start of this project.

I thank you so much for your willingness to add your expertise to this book project.

Please visit Songline Emu Farm where this book took shape.
Songline Emu Farm
66 French King Highway
Gill, MA 01354
413-863-2700
www.allaboutemu.com/songline-emu-farm

CHAPTER 1

AN EMU BREAKS OUT

Stanley Johnson's on high alert in his farmhouse basement as he checks his hatching boxes for the third time today. Suddenly, a quick wobble catches his eye. The jiggle comes from one of the giant midnight-green eggs behind the hatcher's glass door. Stan's ears tune in for whistles and cheeps, but he hears nothing yet. The eggs look like super-large avocados, but inside are emu chicks that have grown too big for their shells. They feel cramped in the tight space, and they're ready to break out. Stan, clad in jeans and a flannel shirt, keeps tabs on the birthing chicks and tends to all the other birds in his flock as well. He seems to possess a sixth sense about his emus' needs.

Songline Emu Farm has been a family operation since 1995. Stan used to be a dairy farmer. Now he raises the second largest birds in the world, and he loves this new version of farming. The huge birds are an increasingly popular type of livestock* that people raise in most U.S. states and in other countries too.

Dee Dee Mares, with her bouncing brown curls and ready smile, greets people who visit and clues them in about the odd birds at the farm. She's Stan's sister-in-law and a fun teacher. Old and young visitors love hearing her facts and stories. Dee Dee also works with museums, talks with scientists and handles many other behind-the-scenes parts of the farm business.

Spring marks a favorite time of year for Dee Dee and Stan. It's emu hatching season. Last night, that first egg in this batch jiggled. Today, the chick inside uses its beak to poke and jab at its tough, thick covering, and Stan hears it peep.

Think of yourself stuffed inside a basketball. With no room to move, you can guess how a nearly-born emu feels. After hours of pecking and chipping, the hatchling* chisels a hole to the outside. The hole sprouts a crack, then a crack in another direction. The chick thrashes and wrestles, trying to a find a way out. Stan watches the egg rock and tilt as though powered by some invisible force. Suddenly the action stops.

Around noon, the wobbling begins again. The egg rolls partway over, and a piece of shell pops off. Inside, the chick cheeps loudly and then quiet reigns. A couple of hours later, the egg trembles, then moves with quick jerky motions.

SAYING "EMOO" OR "EMEW"

No one knows for sure how the emu got its funny name. One story says that as Portuguese sailors sailed around the globe in the 1400s and 1500s, they picked up the word ema, from an Arabic word for "large bird."

Word of mouth claims that when Portuguese sailors later explored Australia, they spotted the six-foot birds and labeled them with the same name. But some experts think the Dutch arrived in Australia before the Portuguese. Did they bring the name "emu" to Australia? The answer isn't clear yet.

People also don't know how "ema" became "emu," but this word continues to evolve. If a person lives in Australia, he or she probably calls the bird an "emew." In the United States, people hear "emoo" just as often. While both pronunciations are correct, Stan and Dee Dee prefer to say "emew".

More shell pieces crack off, and Stan sees that this baby has its foot stuck in its mouth.

Hatching's hard work that takes a grueling twenty-four hours. The chick must rest often before resuming its struggle. The egg jiggles, flops partway over and loses more shell chunks. The baby emu wiggles and squirms until it frees its

Hatchling with foot in mouth.

Newborn emu naps.

foot. Then all becomes still again.

At last, with an energetic shake-shake, the chick wriggles free. The new bird's wet feathers stick together because of the moist world in which it developed. It's exhausted from breaking out and sags to the floor for a well-deserved snooze.

When it wakens, the infant stretches as though trying to unkink its muscles. It stands up straight and checks out its world for the first time. It's ten to twelve inches tall, which is <u>big</u> for a baby bird. Its feathers have dried and fluffed like a

HOW THE UNBORN EMU CHICK GETS ITS FOOD

Inside the fertile* emu egg, a tube connects the emu chick embryo* to its egg yolk. This pipeline delivers nourishment from the yolk sac into the developing baby. As the chick grows larger, its yolk sac becomes smaller. In emus eggs, scientists call this tube the chorioallantois* (kor-e-o-el-lan-toe-is). In unborn human babies, they call it the umbilical cord* .

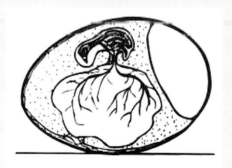

Maria Minnaar

new cotton ball, and handsome brownish-black and cream stripes mark a trail from head to tail. In the wild, this camouflage helps protect it from predators*, but on the farm, the chick is safe.

Stanley cradles the soft bird in his hands. He carries it to a wooden crate that holds hatchlings from other batches. Heat from an electric light bulb keeps the chicks warm, and fresh-smelling wood shavings cover the floor. His new chicks hang out in their cozy nursery for about three days.

They drink from a shallow pan of water on the floor, but they're not hungry. Why? While each baby developed, it received its food from the yolk of its egg. After it hatches, the new emu finishes digesting the yolk. Only then does the baby feel hungry. When the yolk is gone,

---

CHOWING DOWN IN THE OUTBACK
and
FANTASTIC FARM FOOD

The original home of all emus lay in the wild and fertile parts of Australia. There, they could run for miles, and find plentiful food and water. Even today, the emu play-ground-of-choice is the Australian outback* (rural countryside, away from people and towns).

Here they fill up on seeds, flowers, new green shoots and fruits that are in season. They particularly like the sweet red or blue fruit that grows on the Australian quangdong* tree. (Some people call it "wild peach.") Emus also gulp down large insects like grasshoppers and dragonflies. They love caterpillars and munch on small animals like mice or lizards. They even dine on carrion* (dead animals).

There's one more thing an emu eats that most people don't think about. The bird swal-lows stones about a half-inch in diameter. They fall into its gizzard*, a muscular pouch near its stomach. The stoney lumps and the gizzard work together, a bit like a person's teeth. They massage hard-to-digest plant leaves and stems into small bites. The broken-down food then moves to the bird's stomach for further digestion. All birds, including emus, have gizzards.

At Songline, the birds still nibble on insects and mice. But the main course is a feed that arrives in pellet form. It contains a mix of grains like corn, soybeans and wheat. Experts know this adult food provides the perfect blend of plant proteins*, vitamins, minerals and fats that ratites* (flightless birds that include the ostrich, emu, rhea, cassowary and kiwi) need as they grow. Stan and Dee Dee believe their strong, healthy emus do best on this vegetarian* mix.

Protein helps build and repair body tissues like muscles. Minerals like calcium add strength to bones and create thick, sturdy egg shells. Vitamins help the emu's body make effi-cient use of what it eats. Fat supplies energy, and some farmers believe it adds flavor to the food.

the small opening where this food entered the chick's body closes. The tiny spot becomes the baby emu's belly button.

During those first three days, Stan examines the chicks to learn who the males and females are. He weighs the birds and records the number. Then he fastens a colored plastic piece with an ID number to each chick. His tool looks like a pricing gun stores use to tag clothing. "Tagging doesn't hurt the chicks," says Dee Dee. "It's like getting your ear pierced."

When the weather is right, Stan totes the box of striped young-sters to a small greenhouse* in the yard. It's their next step to life out-doors, and it's where they first taste adult emu food that looks like

Tagged and ready to grow.

pellets. Their new food and their new greenhouse home are solid steps toward growing up.

Without hesitation, the striped birds munch down on their first pellets.

Stan's fiberglass* greenhouse soaks up the sun's rays. People make fiberglass by mixing melted glass fibers with plastic. The result can't shatter the way glass can, and you can't see through it. The translucent* material spreads out the sun's direct rays into a gentler light that passes through the walls. During the day, the filtered sunlight brightens the inside. The sun's heat also seeps through the walls. It warms the greenhouse the same way a sunlit room becomes toasty. At night, the greenhouse gradually cools, and the chicks begin adjusting to the change.

"If it's a cold spring, the chicks might live here until they're about two months old," says Stanley. At the same time, he knows it's smart to shoo them out into the cold for ten to fifteen minutes a day. The birds scoot about to keep warm. This tones their muscles and helps them thrive in various weather conditions.

"But, if it's sunny and in the 50s, I keep the chicks outside all day," Stan continues. At three months, the birds are hardy* enough to stand hot and cold temperatures. And they've sprouted to two feet tall.

Stan erects a fence around a grassy area. He's knows the birds can't fly away. Their wings are too small for their bodies and always will be. He builds the sides high enough so the emus can't leap over, but just as important, enemies like dogs or coyotes can't sneak in. During the next three months, the young emus spurt to four and a half feet tall. Their pens become too small and the walls too short for safety. Stan moves them again.

The birds are changing so rapidly, it seems they're in a hurry to grow up. Already, the emus are trading their fading stripes for new black feathers. These poke out on their heads and necks, and finally on their bodies. It's a dramatic shift that makes them easy to spot.

The color change sends a signal to Stan and Dee Dee. They need to take action now to protect the youngsters' good health. They give shots with a medicine that worms the birds. It gets rid of tiny animals you can't see with your naked eye. They live in the bird's intestines and can make them sick and weak. Veterinarians* (animal doctors) call them parasites*.

Adolescent emus in color transition.

"We give a booster shot every year to all the emus we keep for breeding." says Stanley.

Like all teenagers, the leggy birds spring to their adult height in a flash. Suddenly, they're five to six feet tall, and they've shed their black feathers for adult gray-brown plumes. Some even sport a radiant blue patch on the skin of their featherless necks. Their new adult look means they're old enough to have chicks of their own. The partners know there's one more important thing to do to keep their flock healthy.

They inject a second medicine to protect the emus from a deadly disease some people call E.E.E. or "Triple E." Scientists refer to it by its full name: Eastern Equine Encephalitis* (eh-kwine en-ceff-a-li-tis). It exists mainly in the eastern United States.

"This illness moves swiftly," says Stan. "It can kill a small farm's entire flock in one day, and I can't afford to take that chance." Inoculating the birds prevents the possibility of an outbreak.

Stanley strives to give his birds the best care. He's smart and figures out ways to save himself time and energy as he works. He's constructed a water pipeline that runs downhill from the farm house. It stops at each pen where Stan's installed a spigot* (faucet) and placed a drinking tub. There's no need to lug water to the birds by the bucketful. That would be <u>way</u> too much work. Each emu drinks at least one to two gallons per day, and as much as four gallons a day in hot weather. Providing the birds with plenty of clean water is an important part of their care.

"I pay more attention to the birds' water in winter than I do in summer," Stanley says. In cold weather, he drains the waterline each evening so it won't freeze and split the pipe. In the morning, he turns it on and refills the drinking tubs in each pen.

He also places a heater coil in each tub to keep the birds' drinking water from icing up. That method works well, but the birds drop food bits into the water when they drink. The pellets disintegrate, and the tubs get dirty. Bacteria* (germs) grow quickly in the warm water, and it begins to smell bad. "That can't be good for the birds," says Stan, "so I wash the tubs every three or four days, and I disinfect them with bleach once a week." Stanley's standards are high. Emus didn't get this kind of pampering many millions of years ago.

19

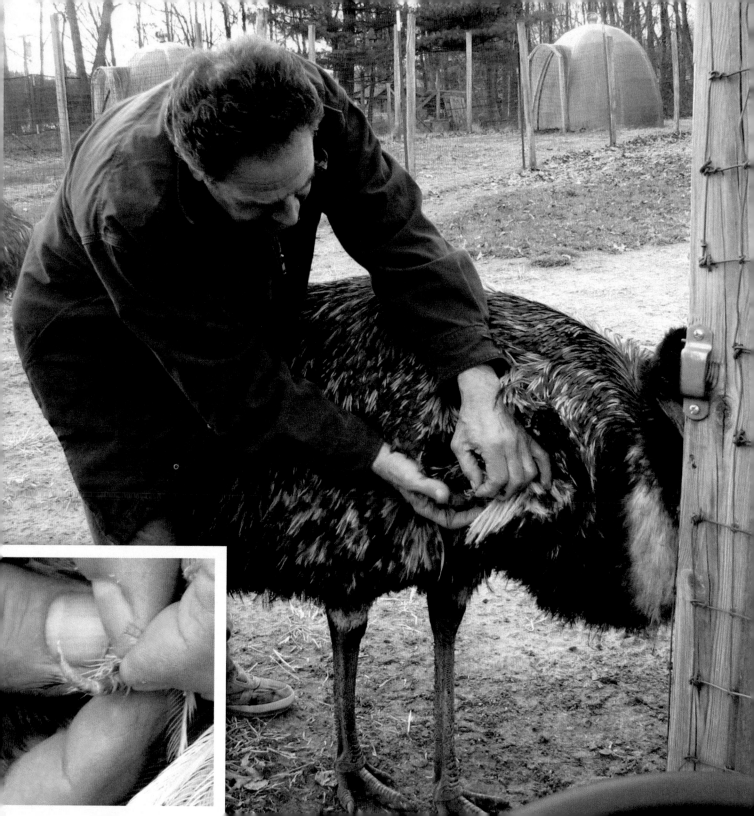

CHAPTER 2

STRANGE CONNECTIONS

SOLVING THE PUZZLE

Do you think today's gentle emu is related to the mighty dinosaur *Tyrannosaurus rex*? Come follow the zig-zag trail to find the answer. It starts in 1861 when German scientists discovered the unbelievable *Archaeopteryx (ar-ke-AP-ter-iks)* fossil. The name meant "ancient wing," and these scientists had never seen a fossil containing such a strange combination of animal types.

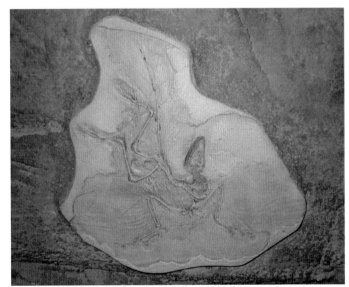

Mold of *Archaeopteryx fossil.*

Springfield Science Museum

Thomas H. Huxley

When the exciting news reached England, Thomas H. Huxley, a well-respected biologist, hurried to examine it for himself. He noted that the strange fossil had a wishbone, wings and feathers like a bird. But it also displayed teeth and a long tail like a reptile. How odd.

His friend, naturalist Charles Darwin, had devised a new theory on evolution that fit *Archaeopteryx* perfectly. Darwin had concluded from his studies and observations that creatures changed a bit with each new generation. Halfway between bird and reptile, nature trapped this example in stone for all to study.

THOMAS HUXLEY: A MAN AHEAD OF HIS TIME

Tom Huxley became the seventh of eight children born into his middle-class family in England on May 4, 1825. Young Tom studied for about two years at the same school where his father taught, but when the school closed, ten-year-old Tom had to leave. His father became unemployed and the family fell on hard times, but that didn't slow Tom down. He was hungry to learn and read everything he could put his hands on.

By adulthood, T.H. Huxley had taught himself German, Latin and some Greek. He knew much about religion and philosophy. Huxley apprenticed to a surgeon at a local hospital, received a scholarship to Charing Cross Hospital and later served as an assistant surgeon on the British ship, the HMS Rattlesnake.

Tom became an early zoologist and very knowledgeable about both vertebrates* and invertebrates* (animals with backbones and those without.) He worked with the great naturalist Charles Darwin, supporting his theory on evolution, while testing it on his own. Tom had had no formal schooling since age ten, yet he became one of the most learned men of his time in England.

Back home, Huxley introduced other scientists to all he'd learned about *Archaeopteryx* and evolution, and explained how this information applied to dinosaurs. But these men of learning didn't believe him. They knew birds were warm-blooded* (endothermic)* like mammals, and they believed all dinosaurs were cold-blooded* (exothermic)* reptiles. Being related didn't make sense to them. They needed proof.

One hundred years later, Dr. John H. Ostrom, a U.S. paleontologist*, literally dug up that proof. In 1964, while searching for fossils in Montana and Wyoming, Dr. Ostrom stumbled on the stony remains of a meat-eating dinosaur never seen before. He carefully brushed dirt away from the remarkable specimen* and found it to be about the size of a wolf or a mountain lion.

The little dinosaur had stood upright and walked on its hind legs, but it was the vicious curved claw hooking out from each foot that caught Ostrom's attention. The hooked toe

Dr. John H. Ostrum with statue of *Deinonychus* in background.

Suzanne DeChillo/New York Times/Redux

Left hind foot of *Deinonychus antirrhopus* (Ostrum 1969).

A special tendon allowed this sharp toe to rise into a deadly slashing position.

CC BY SA 3.0 Private Collection/WikiMedia Commons

sliced into its prey with deadly accuracy. Five years later, Ostrom named this beast *Deinonychus* (dye-NON-ik-us), meaning "terrible claw."

Deinonychus antirrhopus (Ostrum 1969)
Private collection/WikiMedia Commons

Scientists think *Deinonychus* dinosaurs worked in packs, taking down animals much larger than one small dinosaur could handle. Once the ferocious wolf-sized dinosaurs burned up the calories from one meal, they were ready to hunt and eat again. This aggressive lifestyle and need to eat frequently convinced Ostrom that *Deinonychus* and other theropods* (meat eaters) operated with a high metabolism* (their food quickly converted to energy). He also believed they were warm-blooded, since their active lifestyle ruled out the slow, slogging behavior of a cold-blooded reptile.

CLAWS THEN AND NOW

Meat eaters like *Deinonychus* used the claws at the ends of their hands to clutch their prey and tear it apart. As some dinosaurs evolved over millions of years, their hands and fingers changed slowly into wings. As wing evolution moved forward, many birds learned to glide and finally fly. As flyers, they no longer needed their slashing claws, which eventually vanished.

By showing claws on its wings, *Archaeopteryx* illustrates the overlap between birds and reptiles*. (Stanley points out the little claw on the emu's tiny wing. It's a leftover from its dinosaur days. See inset on page 20).

In the late 1960s, he traveled to Germany as Huxley had done, where he compared his *Deinonychus* with the 150-million-year-old primitive bird, *Archaeopteryx*. A delighted Ostrom discovered 22 similarities that linked the bird and dinosaur fossils. Pooling his information, he wrote a new article where he told scientists that meat-eating dinosaurs *were more like non-flying birds than they were like lizards.*

Ostrom also believed feathers appeared on the transitional* creatures before wings developed, and announced to scientists that small *meat-eating dinosaurs grew feathers to keep warm.* Most paleontologists laughed at Ostrom's theories, and the argument raged for more than 20 years. In 1996, a discovery in China changed everything.

WHO WAS JOHN OSTROM?

Born in 1928, John Ostrom grew up in New York City. When he graduated from Union College, he planned to become a doctor like his dad. Then John read a book about evolution and changed his mind, deciding to pursue paleontology instead. He returned to school and graduated with a Ph.D. from Columbia University. For several years, Dr Ostrom taught about prehistoric creatures at the college level.

In 1961, he came to Yale University, where he taught classes, helped manage the Peabody Museum of Natural History and did research on dinosaurs. In 1964, he discovered *Deinonychus*. During the 1960s and 1970s, scientists finally listened to Dr. Ostrom. They learned a whole new way to think about dinosaurs, their traits and their links to modern birds.

Farmers unearthed a 130-million-year-old fossil of *Sinornithosaurus* (sin-ORN-i-tho-saurus)—a knee-high dinosaur with a long, hard-to-pronounce name. Like *Deinonychus*, it sported a nasty claw on each foot, and scientists could <u>see</u> the beginnings of feathers all over its body.

Why was it growing feather fuzz if it couldn't fly? Scientists thought about the climate* at that time. It was warmer than the 21st century, but like now, the weather varied. They decided the fine covering served as a shield that sealed out heat when the weather was too warm. When the weather was too chilly, the same primitive feathers protected like a sweater and locked in body heat. In both cases, scientists decided the newly developing fuzz insulated* the bird, protecting it from uncomfortable conditions.

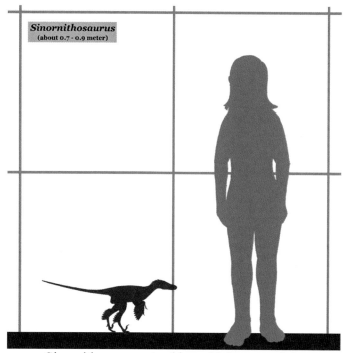

Sinornithosaurus stood knee high to an adult.

Conty/WikiMedia Commons

Wow. At last, the scientific world had its proof, and Ostrom's work answered the question: Are emus and *T-rex* related? Absolutely!

Dr. Manning discovered this three-foot wide print in Montana in 2006. He thinks it belongs to *T-rex* or *Nanotyrannus**.

Dr. Phil Manning

Three-toed emu feet.

The earth and its creatures continued developing and changing as the climate introduced new challenges. Dinosaurs lived on until they could no longer adjust; then they died out. Birds, however, got an "A" for adapting from their dinosaur roots. Their bodies evolved with traits that fit their environments and food sources. Some learned to soar, but for others, physical changes made flight impossible.

Scientists named one group of non-flying birds Ratites*. The word "ratite" referred to the bird's flat sternum* (breastbone). The emus belonged to this group. They couldn't fly, but to make up for this defect, they developed long sturdy legs designed for walking and running. Very few creatures could challenge the emus' speed and quick moves. They reigned in Australia for millions of years, but around 40 thousand years ago, a serious predator arrived.

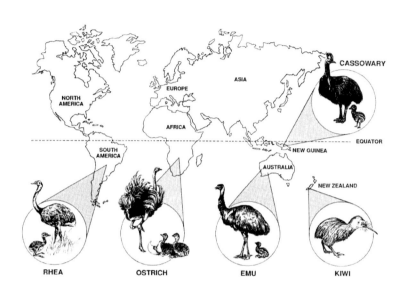

Map showing natural distribution of ratites throughout the world.

Maria Minnaar

28

A CRAZY KEEL BONE AND FUNNY FEATHERS

Why can some birds fly while others are stuck on the ground? It all depends on the bird's flying equipment. A flyer's sternum comes with a special bone that sticks out like the keel on a boat. Its flight muscles anchor themselves here.

When the bird takes off, its specially designed feathers provide lift and the ability to land smoothly. What you notice is the feather's flat part, called a "vane". Each feather contains hundreds of hair-like threads that grow from the feather's main shaft, and each thread contains many microscopic hooks that hold the threads together. Together they form a soft, solid surface. Vanes help a bird soar, and when it lands, its special wings fold neatly around its body.

An emu can't compete with a flying bird, because it's built with a different design. Its smooth breastbone is shaped like a raft and contains no keel. With no place for flight muscles to attach, the bird has evolved without those muscles. It's forever stuck on the ground. Other traits add to its unique-ness.

An emu's feathers can't form vanes, because the tiny hooks are spaced too far apart. They can't interlock with the threads that grow from its main shaft. As you observe the bird, you see long loose plumes that look more like hair than feathers. They seem to float or bounce as the bird walks. And there's yet another amazing difference. An emu is the only bird that produces <u>two</u> plumes from every feather quill on its body.

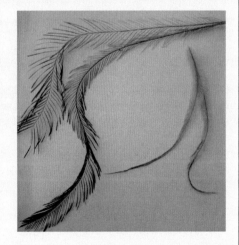

Finally, it seems like a silly accident of nature that an emu's wings measure only eight inches long. That's 1/10th of its body size! Even if an emu had a keel and flight muscles, or if its feathers had vanes, its miniature wings couldn't lift it from the ground.

EMUS AND THE ABORIGINES

Tribes of people were making their way on foot and in crude boats from Asia to Australia. Land masses were much closer then, making such a trips possible. These nomads*, later known as the Aborigines*, explored the land as Australia's first people. As the seasons changed, they wandered to find new sources of food. Men hunted animals; women gathered plants and cared for children.

ABORIGINE BELIEFS

The ancient Aborigines studied the stars and discovered the Emu in the Sky. Its form lay within the dust shadows of the Milky Way. The emu entered other myths and stories, growing out of Aboriginal beliefs about the very beginning of life.

In this "time before time," they were sure that the earth was a flat, monotonous environment with no hills and valleys to add variety to the landscape. Without rivers, there could be no sound of rushing waters, and with no lakes there could be no blue reflected from the sky. In fact, a dull gray saturated everything, and the absence of plants or animals meant there was no life.

These native Australian people called it the Dreamtime and believed their ancestors rose up out of the dust along with plants, rocks, rivers and animals. Sometimes these earliest Australians assigned human qualities to them. They felt everyone and everything was interrelated, and that people were not superior to animals, rocks, water or anything belonging to nature. That thinking meant that emus and people were equal.

In another myth with many variations, Aboriginal tribes tell the story of the first sunrise. They speak about an exploding emu egg and how its giant yolk provided the first light to the earth, revealing its colors and beauty.

Though no one knows when or why, the Dreamtime ended and real life began. After that, the Dreamtime lived on in Aboriginal stories.

In the wild, emus were nomads, too. They trotted along per 30 miles an hour for hundreds of miles in search of green growth. If they felt threatened along the way, the birds would sprint ahead in short bursts at 40 miles per hour. Even though each stride spanned nine feet, their great running skills couldn't match the hunters' ability to outsmart them.

Aboriginal men tracked the long three-toed footprints. They chipped a sharp piece from stone and lashed it to a branch with emu tendons* (tough cords that connect muscles with other parts, like bones). When the hunter hurled this spear, it flew faster than a man could run and reached much farther than his arm could heave a rock. But the clever Aborigines didn't stop there.

Many Aborigines today live as their ancestors did. Note spears and boomerang.

Steve Evans, 2011

About 10,000 years ago, they invented the wooden boomerang* (throwing device). It sliced through the air with deadly accuracy and targeted animals like kangaroos and emus.

The hunters and their families ate the emu's meat, which became a staple in their diets. In ceremonies, they wore its feathers as body decorations. Hides provided strong, long-lasting covers for their bodies, and emu eggshells became drinking cups. The Aborigines used almost every part of the bird.

Today, wild emus still forage* (search for food) in the outback, and they move as the seasons change. Many Aboriginal people continue to live a traditional nomadic life. But there's a big difference between now and 40 thousand years ago. Aboriginal culture now exists side-by-side with a modern Australian population. Some Australians are farmers who, like Stan and Dee Dee, raise emus. Australia now boasts a robust emu farming industry.

EMUS GO INTERNATIONAL

For many years, Australian farmers viewed emus as pests that knocked down their fences, trampled crops and wolfed down their growing grains. The landowners killed the birds that looted their fields, until they discovered that these tall, gawky birds with tiny wings fascinated people in the U.S and other countries. This information provided a solution, and Australian farmers began shipping live emus far away as fast as they could.

Cities purchased the exotic* (foreign, mysterious, different) birds for their zoos, and people bought them for private collections. They also learned the gentle birds flourished in captivity, and with new shipments of birds arriving regularly, breeding emus was easy.

From the 1930s through the 1950s, Australian's continued exporting their fast-running, non-flying curiosities. But in 1960, the emu became Australia's unofficial national bird, and the country passed a new law that made exporting the live birds illegal. This halted the steady supply of new stock to the U.S. and other countries. With fewer birds to choose from, international emu farmers found breeding healthy emus more difficult.

If farmers wanted to be successful, they needed to master the science of raising this new livestock. They talked to each other and read everything they could find about the birds. Farmers then made emu matches based on what they saw, and they learned surprising things about the birds' behavior.

Even today, Stan makes bird matches based on what he observes, his knowledge and experience, and his birds' bloodlines.

CHAPTER 3

THE GREAT ROLE REVERSALS
or
WHO'S THE BOSS AROUND HERE?

Who's the bashful bird? <u>Not</u> the female emu, especially during mating season. When emus pick partners in warm weather (approximately June or July in North America and about December or January in Australia), <u>she's</u> the one who does the choosing. When she spies a male bird she fancies, she fluffs her neck feathers and parades around. If she could talk, she might yell, "Yoo-hoo! Pay attention!" She inflates the large air sac on her neck and burps up a drumming or booming call that sounds like a bongo drum. Her actions seem more like a performance for the stage than a mating dance. If she's successful, the male fluffs his feathers and follows her example. Stanley says he often cocks his head to one side as though looking for her approval.

His air sac is smaller, so the noise he coughs up sounds like a pig's grunt. The two birds walk about eyeing each other, drumming and grunting. They're like two people who date once or twice, and then must decide whether they like each other enough to continue going out. If the birds seem pleased with each other, their prancing performance seals the deal. They remain as a couple until the cold weather (winter in North America and summer in Australia) when the female lays her eggs.

But sometimes a male's not interested in a female's advances. Even though she's taller and weighs more than he does, he still has something to say about the matter. How does he let her know he's not excited about the relationship? He simply walks away.

The female emu doesn't seem bothered by his rejection. Instead, she's immediately on the lookout for another eligible male. Once the female finds a mate, she does something most unusual.

She lays her eggs during the coldest season of the year. In the wild, when the female is ready, the male does all the preparation for her. He digs and scratches a hollow in the ground with his long pointed toes. He tugs at grass with his feet and collects leaves in his beak and lines the hollow. This simple nest shows the female where to put her eggs.

After she lays an egg, the male covers it with some of the grass and leaves, which hides it. This natural insulation helps keep the new egg warm, but not warm enough for the embryo inside to begin growing. Three or so days later, the female adds another egg to the nest. When about eight or nine (called a clutch*) appear in the nest, the male turns into Mr. Mom. From now on, the clutch is his sole responsibility.

WHY EMUS LAY EGGS IN COLD WEATHER

When early emus laid their eggs some 59-56 million years ago, experts think the weather was much warmer and drier than it is today. Emu dads didn't need to keep the eggs warm, because the embryos began to incubate as soon as the females laid their eggs. When hatching time arrived, the hot weather made it hard for the chicks to thrive.

Without an abundant supply of water and fresh green shoots, emu survival rates weren't good. Most of the birds that lived, hatched late in the season. That's when the Australian fall arrived with its cooler, rainy weather. What a relief from the torrid summer heat.

Millions more years passed. Emus gradually shifted their egg-laying time to fall when the days shortened and the weather cooled. These conditions became etched in their DNA, and with chillier conditions, the emu dad followed his instincts. He sat on his clutch, using his body heat to keep the eggs warm. When the embryos matured and the chicks broke out of their shells, they found plenty of water, insects and fresh greens to eat.

Now, wherever emus live, they lay their eggs in the late autumn chill. Below the Equator in Australia, those cool months stretch from May to August. Above the Equator in North America, egg-laying time extends from about late October until March or April.

No one is sure why, but sometimes more than one female lays her eggs in that same nest. Mr. Mom doesn't know or care which eggs are his and which belong to the outsider. He accepts them all. When this happens, Mr. Mom finds himself sitting on as many as twenty giant dark green eggs. The capable fellow doesn't know he's doing double duty now and will be protecting and caring for twice as many chicks after they hatch!

He plants himself on the nest full of eggs for 52 to 56 days, using his body heat to keep them warm. He also protects the clutch from small lizards that like to eat the insides of the eggs. During this "sitting" period, Mr. Mom doesn't eat, drink or defecate* (pass waste). He rises only long enough to turn the eggs several times each day. Instinct* guides him in this important job. He doesn't know it, but he's helping the unborn chicks to develop normally. Turning prevents both the chick embryo and the yolk sac from settling to one side of the egg. Staying centered helps the bird inside grow with well-formed body parts. When Dad finishes turning them, he returns to his seat. Where is Mom while he's working?

No responsibilities.

Once she lays a clutch, that's it! Her job is done. She's a free agent and wanders off. She often finds another male and lays a second clutch. She may even repeat this a third time. It sounds strange, but she can have three males sitting on three nests of her eggs at the same time. And she's able to repeat the process every year for most of her life. That's ten years in the wild and about twenty on the farm. She feels no responsibility to the eggs or later to the chicks. She's "free as a bird."

Meanwhile, back at the nest, Dad settles in for nearly two months of egg-sitting. How does he survive on this starvation diet of no food or water? Before egg-laying time arrives, he uses the warm growing season to fill up on plentiful plants, bugs and small animals. He packs on the pounds and later uses this stored food energy to nourish himself during the sitting time. He needs the endurance it provides as he guards the nest and keeps the egg embryos warm.

Mr. Mom also conserves energy by easing into a trance-like state. He almost seems asleep, but rouses himself easily when he hears noise, senses danger or needs to turn the eggs.

Notice newborn under Dad's beak.

Even so, Mr. Mom's a lot thinner when the eggs hatch. He weighs about sixty pounds instead of his normal ninety. As soon as the chicks hatch, he immediately gulps down their shells. Guided by instinct, he doesn't know this action serves two purposes. First, it quickly destroys the evidence that the chicks have hatched, thus protecting them from predators. And secondly, it jolts his sleeping digestive system to life. He hasn't eaten in almost two months. Now, he can start filling his stomach again and begin to regain his lost weight.

He needs that food energy to meet his chick-raising responsibilities. He teaches his youngsters how to run in a zig-zag pattern. In the wild, this silly-looking strategy helps them escape eagles that dive from the sky to snatch them for a meal. Dad also demonstrates how they can outsmart an attacking feral* (wild) cat or a dingo* (reddish brown wild dog of Australia). While running away, Dad lifts one tiny wing and drops the other. Without losing speed, he pivots sharply, and charges off in a new direction. The enemy must slam on its brakes to slow down before it can turn and resume the chase. Meanwhile, Dad has scooted far out of range.

Mr. Mom schools the young birds in foraging (searching for food). The youngsters learn where to search out tasty plants. They discover how to snap a dragonfly out of the air and flatten a fleeing mouse with a foot. Mr. Mom hovers around his brood until they're 18 months old. They're teenagers now and able to care for themselves. When they reach two years of age, they're grownups and ready to mate.

On the farm, emu life runs by different rules. The female still wants to choose her mate, but at Songline, Stanley plays matchmaker. When he observes a female strutting up and down the fence line, eyeing a male in the next pen, he understands why she's behaving that way. Will he allow them to pair up? He must study the breeding records before he makes that decision. If the two birds are too closely related, he finds a more appropriate mate.

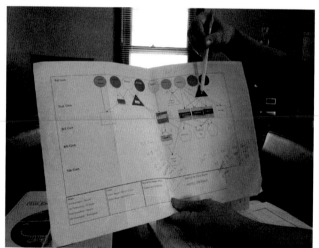
Diagram shows how Dee Dee uses the "rule of threes" to find bird matches.

Dee Dee makes it easier to identify that better match. She tracks the birds' bloodlines* (family histories) from one generation to the next on her computer. Dee Dee knows who's related to whom and how closely.

"When we started Songline," says Dee Dee, "we bought totally unrelated birds from many different bloodlines. We chose carefully to be sure of their health and histories." Today, Songline relies on its own collection of bird histories as the partners continue to build their flock's quality. Occasionally, they select a new unrelated bird to add to the flock.

"This is the part of hatching and raising I find the most interesting," she says. "We breed the birds with the most desirable traits. We want to carry the best features of the emu parents into the next generation." Stanley searches for birds whose feet are set far apart (a wide stance*). He also knows potential breeders should have full bodies and shorter legs. These body builds make for great egg layers.

Routine human contact with emus helps them be comfortable with people.

Stan and Dee Dee also keep an eye out for birds with pleasant dispositions.

"It's fascinating," she says. "There's so little research to look at. For instance, no one knows how long you can refrigerate eggs and still hatch healthy chicks. No one knows, for sure, how closely you can breed emus before you run into body deformations and other difficulties. We do know birds are healthier if they're not too closely related."

How close is too close? Songline uses the "rule of threes." There must be three generations separating a pair of birds before the partners can consider breeding them. This rule has worked well for the farm, yet Stan and Dee Dee don't yet fully understand the science behind it.

"Finding the best matches between birds in our flock gets complicated," says Dee Dee. She uses her computer and lays out potential couples on paper. Meanwhile, Stanley observes the birds outdoors.

"He's the real expert. He knows bird behavior, and he carries a lot of the information in his head," says Dee Dee. "Emus are like people. Every one of them is different." Stan knows who's timid and who's bold, who's got spindly legs and who's well built. Most of all, he understands how the birds' instincts influence their lives in captivity. He's very aware that playing cupid with emus can be tricky business. But with his 17 years of emu-raising experience, he's ready to try a little psychology to get some reluctant birds to like each other.

"There are no guarantees that the two birds we put together as a couple will accept each other," says Stan. He tries two of them in a pen that's as far as he can get from the noisy road. "They seem to need privacy and no distractions to get to know each other," Stan continues. "If they bicker, I separate them with a fence. This lets them get familiar with each other while not being in the same pen."

After a short period, Stan reunites them. Often, time is all they need to decide that this pairing will work for them. But if they still squabble, he returns them to separate quarters. Then he tries one more thing.

"They both need food, and I arrange things so they have to share the same container of ratite pellets," he says. "Sharing their food can bring them together. But if nothing I do works out, I try another bird combination."

Once two emus do accept each other, they mate and she lays her eggs. Because she has no nest, instinct plays a role in where she lays them.

"We might find them anywhere in the pen, even sitting in the snow," says Dee Dee.

Stan agrees, but says, "The females almost always lay in the domed shelters."

Not a stay-at-home mom, the female emu lays her clutch then sashays off without a care.

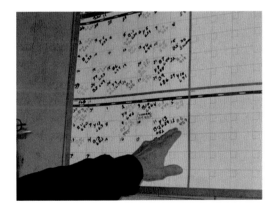

Perhaps the huts with chopped-up leaves for bedding are the closest thing to nests that the females can find.

"All the females tend to lay in the late afternoon and early evening," Stan continues. "Each female is on her own three-day laying schedule, so we make a chart that tells us who's laying on which days. That way, when we collect the eggs, we know which pens to look in and which ones to skip. Each night we pick up the eggs promptly so they don't freeze."

When Dee Dee collects eggs, she uses a box that Stan's invented for that purpose. She carries the dark green ovals to the farmhouse cellar where she weighs them and records the weights in a notebook. This is where the eggs' detailed record keeping begins. Dee

Styrofoam partitions separate the eggs in the egg collecting box.

Dee sticks colored tape on the eggs that tells who the mothers are, and she gives the eggs identifying numbers.

"If two females have eggs in the same pen, Dee Dee and I can tell them apart," says Stan. "Each female's eggs are slightly different in size, shape, color or texture. Finally, it's into the fridge with them." This seems like an odd thing to do with the eggs. Why would Stan and Dee Dee rescue them from the wintry cold only to stash them in a chilly refrigerator?

"The refrigerator's the perfect place," says Dee Dee. "It's 40 degrees inside, so the eggs can't freeze. At the same time, that temperature's too chilly for chick embryos to develop. The fridge puts the eggs on hold until we're ready for them to hatch in the spring."

Sugar Maple Emu Farm

A "large" hen's egg measures two to two and a half inches long and weighs about two ounces. An emu egg measures five to six inches long and weighs about one and a half pounds. One emu egg equals about ten large hen's eggs.

CHAPTER 4

THE MECHANICAL MR. MOM

What if someone asked you to babysit for 50 emu chicks that had recently hatched? Would you find tending to that many scooting, scrambling, ten-inch-tall birds a recipe for trouble? Stan and Dee Dee know the challenges well. And they've designed a plan that reduces stress on the chicks and themselves. They remove eggs from the fridge, one batch of twelve at a time, and allow them to warm to room temperature.

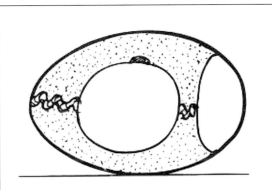

Freshly laid egg with fertilized blastodisc (on top of yolk). Egg not tilted.

Maria Minnaar

The newly formed embryos in the eggs are definitely alive, but like a video on "pause," they seem frozen in time. Unable to generate their own body heat, they can't grow and develop. They crave added warmth to trigger their biological clocks.

Stan and Dee Dee rely on an incubator* to supply the exact temperature the eggs need. It takes the place of father emu, and it's no accident that this heated cabinet warms to 97.5 degrees. That's the same temperature as Dad's nest when he's sitting on a clutch.

The partners place the first batch of eggs into the incubator. A week later a second one goes in, and a week later a third, continuing until the incubator is full. This procedure insures that each batch matures a week after the previous one. Stan and Dee Dee program this automated chick factory to supply everything a growing embryo needs.

Songline's incubator: a large cabinet for growing embryos.

The tiny life in each egg requires a generous supply of oxygen* in order to grow. In nature, the father emu sits on his clutch outdoors where fresh air is all around. Air passes freely through tiny pores* (super small openings) in the egg's thick dark green shell. As the chick embryo takes in oxygen, its muscles, internal organs, feathers and other parts grow and develop. As this happens, the embryo produces used-up air that contains carbon dioxide*. This waste air flows back through the pores in the shell to the outside.

In the farmhouse cellar, there's no outdoor breeze to bring fresh air to the eggs, and the cabinet door remains latched to hold in the incubator's warmth. The embryos still draw in oxygen through their shells, and they continue to release carbon dioxide as waste air. The air around the eggs gets used up, and the developing chicks need more fresh air. The incubator solves the problem by replacing the waste air with new oxygen-rich air it pumps in from outdoors. The embryos develop as well or better than they would under Mr. Mom's body.

The incubator also monitors the correct amount of humidity* (moisture in the air) for the chick embryos. The same pores that let air enter and leave the egg also allow moisture to pass through. Moisture inside the egg evaporates* (changes from liquid form to a gas) and exits through its shell. Because all emu eggs lose moisture, they also lose weight. Losing weight may sound alarming, but this is a normal process.

The tricky part is losing the right amount of moisture. A chick that incubates with too little humidity in the air is like a partially dried out kitchen sponge. When born, the newborn is smaller than it should be. The dry interior of the egg poses another complication to breaking free. As the chick struggles to be born, it may stick to the lining of its shell, making it more difficult to get out. On the other hand, too much humidity causes other problems. Because moisture leaves the egg too slowly, the unborn chick becomes soggy with extra fluid, and its air sac is too small. This chick may not live.

Stan says, "We use a humidity setting of 30 percent on our incubator. That's a good balance between too much and too little moisture." He's confident Songline's chicks will mature in a healthy way.

When Stan or Dee Dee pull the incubator drawers out, the temperature and humidity decrease.

The incubator does another job that the male emu does by instinct. It turns the eggs on steel rollers to keep the yolks centered in their shells. Since each growing embryo is attached to its yolk, rolling the eggs keeps the embryo centered too. Songline's incubator rolls the eggs a half turn in the same direction every half hour.

In the wild, eggs need about 52 to 56 days before they're ready to hatch, but incubator eggs need only about 50 to 52 days. Why? In the nest, the eggs may cool a bit when the Mr. Mom rises to turn them. Sometimes after turning them, he doesn't reposition them under his body completely. Or he may shift to a more comfortable position just as a chilly breeze shivers over the eggs.

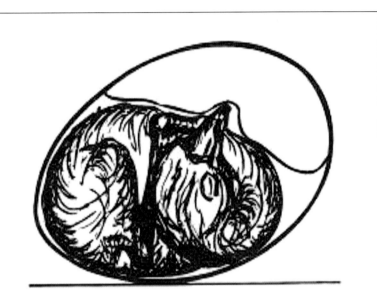

Chick just prior to internal pip. Inner membrane starting to lie down over chick. Air space causing very noticeable tilt to egg.

Maria Minnaar

The mechanical Mr. Mom provides near-perfect conditions. The chicks are fully formed in 34 days, but they need the remaining time to grow to their full size. As hatching time approaches, the shell becomes a tight fit for the growing emu. When the bird was smaller, it could stretch and find a new comfortable position in its shell. That time has passed.

Stanley does two odd tests to determine how close a chick is to breaking out of its shell. He sets two eggs from the incubator on a table, and he whistles to them. One egg remains silent, but the other egg hears and cheeps or whistles in response. How can an unborn chick cheep? There's an air sac at one end of its egg. It's the lighter end and causes the egg to tilt upward. As the cramped chick jostles in its shell, it pips* (pops)

Chick in hatching position, having pipped internally and now occupying the entire space of the egg. Yolk sac almost all drawn in through navel. Egg no longer tilted.

Marla Minnaar

the air sac with its beak and breathes its first air. That's when it can cheep. The bird sprawls into this new-found space, and the egg sits level on the table. This emu is ready to enter the world.

Stan then performs a second easy test. He taps both eggs with a large nail. The silent egg sounds as though he's tapping on a china plate, while the cheeping egg produces a more solid "thud" sound. Stan knows the cheeping egg is ready to break out of its shell, so he transfers it to the hatching box*, a mini incubator of sorts. He returns the quiet egg to the big incubator where it can continue to grow.

As Stan and Dee Dee monitor the closest-to-hatching batch of eggs, they must open and close the big incubator door frequently. The open door cools the incubator's temperature below the perfect 97.5 degree mark, which endangers the embryos in newer batches.

Hatching box, with its glass door open.

The hatching box solves this big problem by allowing Stan and Dee to pay close attention to the nearly-born chicks, while the younger embryos remain safe and warm in the incubator. Smaller than its big cousin, the "hatcher" pumps in fresh air and maintains nearly the same temperature, but it has no steel rollers. Stan doesn't need to worry about keeping the birds centered within their shells, because they've grown so big that they fill up that space. As he and Dee Dee await the arrival of Songline's newest emu generation, they toss around some big questions: Can a modern emu "remember" what its ancestors did? Is that information in its genes? What would happen if one of their farm-raised birds sat on a clutch of eggs the same way its ancestors did in the wild, millions of years ago? Neither partner has a good answer to any of these questions, so they decide to do an experiment.

INCUBATORS FOR OTHER IMPORTANT JOBS

Sometimes a human baby is born too soon. Doctors place the tiny being in a clear glass or plastic box called an incubator in the hospital's nursery. This container keeps the infant warm and protects it from germs and noise. Because the incubator imitates conditions in the mother's body, it gives the baby more time to grow and develop. Nurses feed and care for the child until it can thrive outside this protective device.

A second type of incubator provides excellent growing conditions for bacteria. A medical lab worker draws a small amount of blood from a sick person and places the blood sample in a specially prepared Petri dish* (a shallow circular dish with a loose fitting cover.) She inserts the dish into a special heated box. After a specific amount of time, she checks the dish. If bacteria have multiplied, the lab worker can see the growth in the dish. She identifies the bacteria, and a doctor prescribes the correct medicine to help the person get well.

Other scientists, called entomologists*, use insect growth chambers to study insects that attack fruits and vegetables. One fruit enemy is the Rosy Apple Aphid. It sucks sap from apple leaves, making them curl and dry out. It also causes apples to be too poorly shaped to be sold. The Mexican bean beetle feasts on the leaves of green bean plants. When the chomping chewers finish, only the lacy leaf skeletons remain. Without leaves, the plant can't use the sun's energy to help produce beans. Entomologists find natural ways to control these food pests. In one case, a fungus grows on the insect's body and kills it.

Some incubators aren't machines. Seeds sprout quickly in the warm, moist soil of a garden. Can you think of another kind of incubator?

CHAPTER 5

NATURE'S WAY

Selecting an emu to star in their test becomes the first challenge. Dee Dee points out that Gomer is one of Songline's best breeding males. He's fathered many chicks that share his gentle personality. This trait must be in his genes. Stanley comments that Junior Johnson is another possibility. He's younger than Gomer, well built, a successful breeder and has an easy-going disposition. Gomer and Junior Johnson have lived only on the farm. They have no clue how

Dee Dee and Gomer. Emus often form affectionate relationships with their owners.

wild emus behave. Neither one has ever scratched out a hollow and lined it as a nest for a female. The two male emus have never "sat" on eggs for almost two months. The incubator eliminates that job. And finally, these adult birds have never raised the chicks they would have hatched.

To be on the safe side, Stan and Dee Dee decide to use Gomer <u>and</u> Junior Johnson in their experiment. Two birds mean two chances to remember. They give the birds a colossal hint by building each male a nest lined with hay or leaves in a shelter of his own. It's like having private bedrooms. The nests show the emus where to "sit," and the huts shield the inquisitive birds from distractions that might get them up from their sitting jobs.

JUST TO BE DIFFERENT…

How does a female emu pop out a chalky blue or turquoise egg when most that she lays are dark green? The secret lies in how she forms the shell. Inside her body, egg shell layers build up from the inside to the outside. Closest to the embryo is the white layer. Farther out, shades of turquoise and teal form, getting darker as they near the surface. Greenish black to emerald are the most usual outside colors. Finally, a clear covering seals the egg, providing the very last layer. Then the female lays her egg.

This unusual egg is turquoise and has two yolks—called a double-yolker.

A turquoise egg passes through the female's birth canal before it receives all its layers. It's exciting to know many healthy chicks hatch from blue or turquoise eggs even without their last shell coats.

Next, the partners provide the biggest clue of all. They place a clutch of labeled eggs in each nest. The partners know which females laid them and which breeding males are the real fathers.

Junior and Gomer don't seem to care whose eggs they're sitting on. They simply seem to know that "sitting" is what they're supposed to do. That's a good sign. A few days later, Stan and Dee Dee peek inside. Gomer hears them coming. He hunches his chest forward, protecting the clutch of eggs Stan and Dee Dee selected. It's possible that too much watchfulness could jinx the process, so the partners reign in their cu-

Gomer settles in for his "sitting" period.

riosity. It's not easy, but they go about their normal chores, as patiently as they can, for the next two months.

Finally, the time is up. Did Gomer and Junior remember their ancient roles? Did they remain seated for the 52 to 56 days in their private "bedrooms"?

"Gomer had a short memory," Stan says. "Sometime during the 52 to 56 day period, he got to his feet and walked away." Sadly, none of his eggs hatched.

"On the other hand, Junior Johnson's memory worked perfectly. He remained on the nest for the whole period."

When the time came, Stan peered into Junior's shelter and saw one new chick peeking out from under its father's body. The second day, he found Junior watching over five healthy newborns. Stan checked under Junior's feathers. Was another chick hiding beneath them?

He discovers one egg from the clutch that didn't hatch. "Sometimes these things happen," he says. "Maybe that egg never had an embryo inside

Songline Emu Farm

Songline Emu Farm

it."

"It's interesting to see how this experiment played out," he says. "We can't call it a success or a failure, because it's both." However, he and Dee Dee decide they'll continue to depend on the incubator to hatch their chicks.

"New England weather is too unpredictable," says Stan. "Temperature and humidity can change from day to day, and every year is a little different, too. Our incubator and hatcher take the guesswork out of the process."

The year's hatching season ends when the last chick shakes free of its shell. Stan shuts down the incubator and the hatcher. He and Dee Dee consult to solidify plans that will improve the farm in the coming year, and the two study a drawing that outlines a change in the pens' layout. The new arrangement provides for this year's chicks as they grow. They also discuss which adult birds will become new breeders, which will be sold and which must be processed for meat. Dee Dee tells Stanley that Harvard University is doing a research project using emu egg embryos and wants Songline's help. With so much to talk about and do, it's going to be an exciting year, and Stan, who likes to plan ahead, has his first job lined up already.

How To Move an Emu Safely: Grasp the tiny wings like handles.
Stand behind the emu to avoid forward kicks. Gently propel the bird in the desired direction.

CHAPTER 6

STAN—THE HUMAN EMU DAD

DADDY LONG LEGS

Stanley's shovel chunks into the dense earth, and soon piles of rich-smelling dirt sit next to the holes he's dug. He sinks sturdy wood corner posts into them and stomps soil around each one to hold it in place. Hefty boards follow, which he nails to the posts. To complete the job, Stan staples wire livestock fencing onto the wood. The new pens separate the birds from the outside world and foil a trick the long-legged creatures like to play.

"Because of their long legs, adult emus can jump six feet straight up. That's why their fences need to be at least that tall," says Stan. "They're curious birds, and their urge to roam remains as strong as it was in ancient times." Given the chance, they may vault to freedom just for fun. Younger birds can't jump as high, so they do well in shorter pens.

"<u>But</u> you have to stay alert," he warns. "It's smart to move them to larger enclosures before they outgrow the ones they're in. A few years ago, two birds from a farm near here escaped and ended up on the interstate highway. I'm glad I wasn't the one trying to catch them."

Last year, Stan experimented with a lighter-weight wire that had smaller holes. In a few months it sagged and bent, sending a wrong invitation to the birds. Stan felt lucky no one got away, and he replaced the problem fencing immediately.

A HOUSE ISN'T ALWAYS HOME

Stanley pays attention to many other farming responsibilities besides his emus' pens. The birds' shelters are a good example. He understands that emus adore winter's cold and don't need houses for everyday living the way people do. But he's also aware that when the temperature dips to the single digits or below, the lanky birds need a little help. Stan's domed huts provide an essential barrier to the weather.

Commercial emu shelter with vent..

"The birds seem to know they can keep each other warm," he says. "They huddle close together inside during the day, and at night they curl up to sleep on the shelter's bedding, often with a mate."

Stan says emus also seek protection when blustery wind whistles around the farm. Perhaps the birds don't like having their shaggy feathers tossed every which way. Or maybe they lose body heat when the gusty weather sneaks close to the skin. Either way, the birds don't like wind and seek temporary cover inside Stan's dome-topped huts.

For months, he's been on the lookout for more shelters, and like most farmers, Stan operates on a budget. He's clever and reluctant to buy new if he can find something used that does the trick. He checks every place he knows that stocks used equipment and one day stumbles on a treasure—large, fiberglass containers. People used them at the supermarket to recycle their empty cans and bottles. The store's traded them in for newer models, and Stan knows as soon as he spots them, that they'll work for his birds. He's ready to buy the lot, when he discovers they're free!

RUNNING OUT OF THINGS TO DO?

Stanley spends blocks of time during the summer cutting a "door" into the side of each container so the emus can enter and leave. He also patches the round opening for the bottles

and cans, converting all the fiberglass containers into super shelters for his birds.

"See? New isn't always better", Stan says with a grin,.

He finishes this project and jockeys the domes into the emus' pens as crinkly autumn leaves begin to swirl and collect. Stan chops them with his lawn mower, rakes them into piles and shovels the chipped results into the huts. Recycled leaves provide clean bedding and a layer of insulation between the birds and the frozen ground.

Just as Stan completes a job like fences or shelters, a new season blows into his life with its own excitement. A week ago, one of the female breeders laid her first dark green beauty, thus launching Songline's next laying cycle. Last night, December's first snowfall finished with an icy covering on top.

The tires on Stanley's black pickup chew through the crust in the morning, and carve sharp imprints into the heavy wet snow beneath. The truck, loaded with a ton of emu pellets in 50-pound sacks, groans as it halts by the emus' pens. Stan hops down from his seat and shoulders a 50-pound sack. He lowers it onto a small wagon and piles three more on top. Stan tugs the load through the snow to the nearest red feed bin, where he pours in enough to refill it and heads to the next barrel.

The restaurant that never closes.

These large containers once held pickles, but now they're another example of how Stan saves himself work. Each stores multiple days-worth of crunchy feed, and snap-on lids protect it from moisture. Now he no longer must haul heavy sacks into the pens every day. He knows how much the birds eat and simply scoops enough into smaller feeding barrels he's fashioned. Stan drills holes through the sides, big enough so the emus can stick their heads through and munch whenever they want.

It seems that Stan devotes many hours to this farming job, but he disagrees. "Emus are less work than many other kinds of livestock," he says. "For instance, when I was a dairy farmer, I had to milk the cows every morning and evening, regardless of the weather. If I got sick, I still needed to milk them twice a day."

With emus, it's not a big deal if Stan's not feeling well. Food's already in their feeding stations. If the birds eat everything, they're still all right. In the wild, they go for days without food while they search for a new supply of it.

"On the other hand, some types of livestock keep eating, even if they're not hungry," observes Stan. "That's not healthy, and they get fat. Their farmer must monitor how much food he provides, every time he feeds them. Emus just know when to stop."

Stanley is like an emu dad. He watches over and protects his birds with the same dedication a father emu uses as his chicks grow. But for Stan, this goes way beyond instinct; his mind percolates, planning and making decisions about his flock.

TO NAME HIS BIRDS—OR NOT?

Songline is a small farm, and Stan considers twenty to twenty-five adult birds ideal for the amount of land he has available. He also knows emu farming is a juggling act.

"There are times when I have as many as 40 birds living here, and that's too many," he says. "Forty crowds the pens, but that changes quickly when other farmers pick up the emus they've purchased.

Stan must also balance the number of older and younger emus as one year rolls into the next. He decides which emus stay at Songline and which will be sold or processed. Because the number of birds is always changing, Stan and Dee Dee don't name them. They're farm business, not pets, and sometimes Stanley must make hard choices.

He may decide to process an older female for meat. She's always laid large eggs and produced many healthy chicks. Still, Stanley knows older females lay eggs with thicker, tougher shells. Baby emus fight hard to break out of them, and sometimes the newborns don't survive.

Younger females lay eggs with thinner shells, and their chicks
enter the world with much less struggle.

Stan needs vigorous chicks to continue developing a quality flock. But Stan and Dee Dee do have one exception to their "name" rule. The emus they select to be breeders can live at Songline for many years.

"We talk about them using people's names instead of numbers like B-23 or C-5," says Dee Dee. "Names are easier to remember, and we have fun picking them. Antony and Cleopatra come from history, Bill and Hillary from politics and friendly Gomer from a sweet, funny television star." But whether the huge birds have names or not, sometimes they get goofy.

BEHAVING LIKE KIDS

When emus are in the mood for fun, they leap, run and roll on the ground. They seem to entertain each other with their games and sometimes try to include a person standing nearby. A bird might trot up to Stan, dart away, then run up to him again. It's inviting him to join its game. The long-legged creatures have their own versions of tag, hide and seek and playing

"Hey, wait a minute. Its <u>my</u> turn."

with a ball. They're also excellent swimmers, love to play in water and welcome a good soaking on a hot day.

Many emu farms have ponds where emus can practice their swimming skills. The bird's entire body floats just below the water's surface like a submarine. Some folks think its fat pad and long bushy feathers hold it close to the surface. All you can sees are its head and long neck extending straight up from the water. The bird's head and neck looks like a submarine periscope scouting its surroundings. One emu farmer described the sight as looking like "the Loch Ness Monster cruising across a lake."

Songline doesn't have an emu pond, so when hot weather sets in, Stan or Dee Dee "showers" the birds. When Dee Dee brings out the hose, the birds seem to know what to expect. As she opens the nozzle, they edge closer. She sprays them until they're drenched, and their wa-

terlogged feathers hang low. Soon, the emus look as though they're wearing big heavy overcoats.

Suddenly one shakes, flinging water in every direction like a soggy long-haired dog. Another follows its example. As Dee Dee continues to rain on them with the hose, water collects under their feet. Their gangly legs fold down, and the big birds sink into the puddle as though it's an inviting bath tub. Long feathers settle into the brown water, but the birds don't seem to care. In fact, they're reluctant to rise. This "play" is different from running and jumping. The birds are like people relaxing at the beach or enjoying a spa day. When the emus finally get up, they shake again, soaking everyone and everything.

Dee Dee laughs and wipes water off her arms. "I make sure I never wear white clothes when I'm doing this," she says.

Songline's emus amble off, dry and fluff their feathers and preen* (put their feathers back in order). Dee Dee's done watering the birds, but she's not "done" with her job. She has another exciting project in mind

---

COOL BIRDS

Getting soaked is one way to cool off, but an emu practices other strategies as well:

1. An emu carries a superb insulating system with it at all times. This bird packs almost all its body fat in a pad that sits atop its back. In summer, the cushion shields the emu from the direct rays of the searing sun. (In the winter, it acts like a blanket, slowing the escape of its body heat.)

2. In hot weather, the silly emu pants like a dog. As air moves over its wet tongue, moisture evaporates, and like a dog, the tall bird feels cooler. The technique maintains its body temperature within a healthy range.

3. Under its miniature wings hides another method for staying cool. A mesh of tiny blood vessels covers the surface of its bare underarms. Some farmers think the bird's wings are part of that network too. The bird lifts its wings in hot weather, and air circulates around them. The moving air cools the blood in the network of veins the same way a dip in a pool cools your blood.

CHAPTER 7

REACHING BEYOND THE FARM

Dee Dee's on a mission. Her job reaches well beyond finding good bird matches. She's an emu ambassador* who teaches and builds good will about the emu farming industry. She spreads information as far as she can about these odd-looking birds, their usefulness and their survival story. It's a huge job.

Getting acquainted.

Sometimes Dee Dee totes striped emu chicks to elementary schools. The youngest children pat the fuzzy babies as she introduces them to this unusual breed. Other times, she notifies teachers about the tours she offers at the farm. Older kids learn about dinosaurs in class, then take a field trip to Songline. They handle the birds' leather hides and check out the giant green eggshells. Middle graders learn why these amazing birds can't fly, finger the birds' long wiry plumes and hear their history. Dee Dee intrigues kids with emu factoids and explains that farmers raise this unique livestock for its delicious, healthful red meat and valuable oil, which has healing qualities.

Who is taller?

Dee Dee unlatches the gate to one of the emus' large pens, and the children enter with her to stand near the gentle birds. When the emus extend their necks, they stand taller than the kids. The inquisitive birds sidle up to the two-legged strangers as if wondering who these young creatures are.

One girl wears a shiny red headband in her hair, and its glint captures the attention of a nearby emu. As Dee Dee speaks about the birds, the girl feels something, and her hands fly to her head. She squeals as she discovers her headband is no longer there.

"There it is!" a boy yells. Everyone stares as he points, and they spot the plastic band clamped in the bird's soft broad beak. As the girl shifted from one foot to the other, the playful bird couldn't resist the crimson plastic flashing in the sun. It could just as easily have snatched up a shiny tin can lid gleaming on the ground.

Dee Dee chuckles as she retrieves the headband. She returns it to the girl with a few words about emus' pranks and unstoppable curiosity. She knows the kids will remember this funny part of their trip to Songline.

Spring is a popular time for whole families to arrive on weekends and during school vacations. In the farmhouse base-

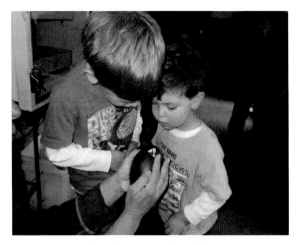
Two boys inspect a hatching egg.

Holding on to the wriggling birds is a challenge.

ment, they see new life emerge from its shell, and it enchants them all. Out on the lawn, the striped babies scurry about. Often a kid or parent scoops up a soft bundle and holds it for a bit. Occasionally, a senior citizen group arrives on a field trip of its own. The seniors are just as curious about emus as the school kids. Dee Dee likes talking to all ages about the birds. She loves to answer people's questions, but she doesn't stop there.

She brainstorms and decides to try something new. Dee Dee knows kids like dinosaurs, so she phones experts at the Peabody Museum in Connecticut and the Springfield Museum in Massachusetts. Would they be interested in hatching some enormous "dinosaur eggs" from her farm?

Hatch those giant eggs in a museum? Who ever heard of such a thing? Wonder turns to approval. The staff at both museums pounce on the idea. They imagine kids and adults watching the big, dark green emu eggs rock, tilt and crack before their very eyes. People would love it.

In the dinosaur department, the museum staff creates a warm, safe spot for the hatching box. Lights shine on the eggs so visitors can see every quiver and shake as the emu chicks break out. One by one the eggs put on a show. Museum dinosaur experts want kids and grownups to see the link between emus and their ancient cousins.

Dee Dee has another thought bouncing around in her mind. She talks with zoo managers at the Zoo in Forest Park in Springfield, MA. She wonders if she and Stan can loan some emus to them. The zoo's staff thinks this terrific plan would allow city kids to see the unusual birds during summer vacation. The emus Dee Dee sends are the very same chicks that hatched this spring, but at three feet tall, they're not "chicks" anymore. Zookeepers provide the birds with a large enclosure where sun dapples through the trees. They post signs with tidbits about these odd birds, and inquisitive visitors pause to study the emus in their zoo surroundings.

"I tell people the emus are at summer camp," Dee Dee says.

Camp ends in November when the Zoo in Forest Park closes for cold weather. The young birds, that now stand four feet tall, have done a terrific job teaching the public about themselves. Stanley trailers them home to Songline where they share the same large fenced-in area with the young birds that hatched under Junior's warm body. Only Stan can tell which is which.

Emu at Forest Park Zoo.

Can you guess how? Their colored ID tags make it clear.

Chilly November announces a new season at Songline: egg-laying time. Junior's chicks and the ones from the zoo aren't old enough to have babies. They need another year to grow. But Stan and Dee Dee will collect eggs from their mature breeders. This lays the groundwork for a new generation of chicks in the spring.

Dee Dee's eager for the season's first dark green egg to appear. But she's also itching for a new project that will leapfrog Songline and the emu industry into the future. Her mind sizzles with ideas.

CHAPTER 8

WHAT LIES AHEAD FOR THIS "DINOSAUR"?

High on Dee Dee's priority list sits a machine that doesn't exist yet. Until now, refrigerators have served to keep emu eggs cool prior to their entering the incubator. And farmers have turned each egg by hand, every day, to keep the yolks and embryos centered. What the industry needs is new equipment that keeps the eggs cool <u>and</u> turns them in a single operation. Dee Dee's applying for a grant to help pay for the development of this new machine.

She also dreams about a communication network for all emu growers in her New England region. Dee Dee is current president of the New England Emu Association (NEEA). She and other members are creating a regional data base of emu farmers.

"This online system will make discussing emu farming so much easier," Dee Dee says. Instead of many individual farmers loosely connected by the breed they raise, she sees them as a closely knit group that can share ideas, solve problems and stay united.

"In addition, the website will be a useful tool that helps other people start raising the birds," says Dee Dee. "Emu farming doesn't take much room or a lot of work. Give the birds some land, shelter, water and nutritious food, and they don't demand a whole lot out of you." Dee Dee's now designing a new program she calls "Emu 101." It teaches new emu growers how to begin and where to seek help when they need it. She'll offer this new course through the NEEA's website, which will be up-and-running soon.

"Good communication is the key to the success of the industry," she says. "Going forward, all emu growers will depend on electronic tools like email and social media for promoting their businesses and educating people about emus and their many excellent products. " Her vision for New England sees many small emu operations, often on the same farms that raise other plant and animal products.

Further, she feels, new and established emu farmers can team up with experts in other fields to expand and promote the emu industry. Dee Dee's phoned the Division of Animal Health at the Massachusetts Department of Agriculture. She knows the U.S. government already considers emus a form of poultry, and she hopes Massachusetts will add a ratite element its poultry program. She's also spoken with staff at the University of Massachusetts Veterinary and Animal Sciences program about areas where they and Songline might work together.

Researchers from some universities are already investigating the science behind emu biology. With help from Songline's incubator, Harvard University is studying the genetic information that spurs an unborn chick's wings to begin forming. Perhaps one day this knowledge will spill over to human studies.

It's amazing how the gentle emu, with its ferocious dinosaur beginnings, is sliding into the 21st century with great ease. Today, people in the U.S. and many other countries use the same emu products that served Aboriginal populations so many thousands of years ago. But science is now opening new avenues for this bird.

"There are so many different directions we can explore," says Dee Dee. What lies ahead for the emu is uncharted territory that's loaded with possibilities.

Can the people who make incubators build one that rolls the eggs and has a chilling unit instead of a heating system? Will inventors design something new? Can the grant Dee Dee's applied for help pay for this development? Time will tell.

BOOMERANG ZOOMERANG

A flying stick swooshes through the air toward its target. It careens around the scrub growth, and shoots toward a kangaroo's knees. The boomerang whacks its target with amazing speed and accuracy, and the kangaroo crashes to the ground with a dull thud. The hunter springs forward with a whoop at his success and the joy of knowing he's captured food for his family.

But before Aboriginal men could fling such a powerful hunting tool, they first had to invent it. Roughly 10,000 years ago, they discovered through much experimentation, that "throwing sticks" traveled farther when cut and shaped from strong, heavy Australian hardwoods like mulga* or sheoak (she oak). They chose curved pieces 24 to 36 inches long and learned to use heat from fire to make the wood even harder. They also used heat to bend the wooden ends to the exact shape for throwing accuracy. They refined their throwing skills, learning to heave this weapon up through the air or close to the ground, and watched as the hunting stick spun end-over-end toward its target. On arriving, it killed or injured animals like kangaroos or emus with a blow to the legs or neck. To fly exactly where the weapon's owner aimed it, this early boomerang had to be perfectly balanced. It didn't return to its owner and wasn't supposed to. What hunter would wait for its return, then carry it back to the animal he'd just slain?

As years passed, the Aborigines discovered that a smaller flat stick with a curve flew on a different path than their heavier hunting weapon. They experimented with the curved design, which required less precision than the hunting boomerang, and they perfected their throwing techniques. Ultimately, Australia's native people created a boomerang that flew into the air when its owner heaved it and zoomed back to him like a yo-yo on a string. In addition, this amazing multi-purpose tool allowed a person to clap two together to send a message or mark a musical beat. He could wave it like a sign to get the attention of others, or dig in the dirt with it. The Aborigines even used this smaller returning version for play and sport, just as people do today.

Many think the boomerang is purely Australian. But people in Egypt, southern India and other countries used boomerangs in other times. In 1987, scientists discovered a boomerang in a cave

in Poland and estimated its age at about 20,000 years old. An ancient person crafted this imple-
ment from a mammoth's tooth.

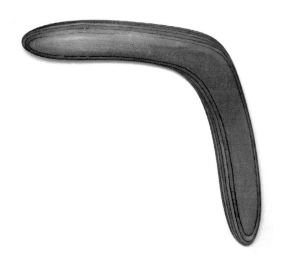

Returning Boomerang

www.boomerangshop.com

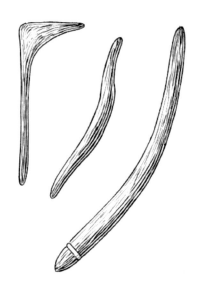

Types of Hunting Boomerangs

Pearson Scott Foresman

WHAT YOU CAN DO WITH EMU

Emu Products as Food

If you're serving an emu egg for breakfast, you'd better invite your friends. That's because one green egg equals ten to twelve hens' eggs. If everyone decides on soft boiled, plan on an <u>hour</u> to simmer that egg. Or you might whip up an omelet or scrambled egg to save some time.

Emu burgers and brats.

Sugar Maple Emu Farm

An emu egg takes care of the first meal of the day, but what do you do at lunch time when your stomach growls again? You might choose a juicy emu burger or cheeseburger. Emu tastes similar to beef, but it's packed with more protein per pound. This helps boost your stamina* (staying power) when you're in action.

Most folks find emu eggs, roasts, steaks, sausages and sandwich meat in organic and natural food stores, but you can also locate these items in a few large supermarkets. If you live in a state with many emu farms, you'll see emu meat and eggs listed on restaurant menus.

Leather

You probably never think about "bird" and "leather" in the same sentence, but the odd emu produces <u>two</u> different skins. Beneath its floppy feathers lies a surprisingly large body hide that could become a kid's vest or jacket. When cured* or tanned (treated to

Sugar Maple Emu Farm

84

last), the skin becomes a soft leather that shows off its handsome quill pattern. (See inset on page 72)

The second showpiece leather grows on the emu's long and speedy legs. Calloused-looking areas protect the bird from scratches and scrapes as it bounds through the grasslands and underbrush of rural Australia. Once tanned, this leather looks like snake or alligator skin.

Leather workers often dye the soft, cured hides with rich colors before creating fashionable items for people. (See page 72)

Emu Oil

Most people think of animal fat as a waste product, but emu growers know a secret. Once refined, the fatty cushion on the bird's back produces five to six quarts of clear oil. It absorbs easily into your skin, helps heal burns and dry itchiness, and soothes aching muscles and joints. The ancient Aborigines rubbed it into their skin to treat these same problems.

Today, some veterinarians apply emu oil and ointment to pets to reduce inflammation from flea bites. It calms inflamed areas that pets gnaw at and irritate more.

Some cosmetics companies blend emu oil into their lipsticks, creams and lotions. A few add it to sunscreens and hair conditioners too.

Many farmers, including Stanley and Dee Dee, sell emu oil skin care products at their farm stores.

Egg Shells

Decorated emu shells go WAY beyond any Easter egg art you've ever seen. Using an electric drill, a crafter bores a small hole through each end of an infertile emu egg, blows out the insides and prepares the shell for fun.

They scratch or carve into the shells. Careful sculpting allows the layers of white, blue, teal and green to peek through to the surface.

Other artists paint pictures or designs on the shell's surface.

According to Joylene Reavis of the American Emu Association, consumers now want more emu products than growers can supply. Farmers are working hard to fill this need.

HOW TO BLOW OUT A HEN'S EGG

1. Have an adult nearby as you perform this task. Hold the uncooked egg securely in one hand. With an ice pick or a long needle in the other hand, carefully poke a small hole through the shell at one end of the egg. Work gently to prevent the thin-shelled hen's egg from breaking.

2. On the opposite end of the egg, repeat the process, producing a slightly larger hole. Be careful positioning the egg on a hard surface as you do this. Pressing down may crush the egg's shell.

3. Insert your poking tool into the larger hole, and stir gently to break up the yolk and the white parts inside.

4. Position the egg over a bowl, large hole down. Blow through the small hole on top until all of the clear egg white and the yolk dribble out. Often the egg white empties first, followed by the yellow yolk. Save the white and the yolk for a cooking project.

5. Rinse the empty shell inside and out. Place it in a small pot of hot water for several minutes to clean the inside of the shell. Carefully remove the shell from the hot water using tongs or a slotted spoon. Allow it to cool and dry.

Piercing an eggshell.

Blowing out the egg's contents.

GLOSSARY

Aborigines—First people to inhabit Australia.

Ambassador— Representative who spreads information and good will about his/her industry, organization or government.

Archaeopteryx—Extinct primitive creature having traits of both birds and reptiles. Like reptiles, it had a long bony tail, teeth and claws at the end of its fingers. Like birds, it had wings and feathers.

Bacteria—Germs. Tiny organisms that can cause illness.

Biologist—Scientist who studies the plant and animal life.

Blastodisc—Newly formed embryo.

Bloodlines—Inherited family traits.

Boomerang—Bent or angled throwing stick. It's usually flat on one side and rounded on the other, so that it soars and curves in flight.

Brood—Family of young animals.

Carbon dioxide—A colorless, tasteless, odorless gas formed especially when breathing.

Carrion—Dead animals.

Chorioallantois—Food tube that connects an emu embryo to its yolk sac.

Climate—Prevalent set of weather conditions existing on a given part of the earth.

Clutch—A nest of eggs.

Cold-blooded—Inability to generate body heat. Having a body temperature that matches the environment.

Cured—Treated or processed to make last. Example: Leather that's been "tanned."

Darwin, Charles—English naturalist, (1808-1882.) His theory of evolution changed the way people see life on earth.

Deinonychus—Small meat-eating dinosaur, about ten feet long and weighing about 170-180 lbs.

Defecate—Pass solid waste from the body.

Dingo—Wild dog of Australia.

Eastern Equine Encephalitis—Illness spread by mosquitoes, often called E.E.E. or Triple E. These mosquitoes bite animals, birds, and even people. Found mostly in the eastern U.S.

Embryo—Animal in the very early stages of life.

Emu—One of five flightless birds known as ratites. The emu is the second largest bird in the world.

Endothermic—Warm blooded.

Entomologist—Scientist who studies insects.

Equator—Imaginary circle around the earth that's the same distance from the north and south poles.

Evaporate—To convert moisture from a liquid to a gas.

Evolution—Theory that explains how plants or animals change over many generations.

Exothermic—Cold-blooded.

Exotic—Foreign, mysterious, different.

Feral—Tame animal that has become wild.

Fertile—Able to grow and develop.

Fiberglass—Material composed of melted glass fibers mixed with plastic.

Forage—To wander in search of food.

Gizzard—Muscular pouch near a bird's stomach. Since birds have no teeth, they swallow small stones. The stones stay in the gizzard and help to grind up food before it's digested.

Guongdong tree—Australian tree with shiny sweet red or blue fruit and an edible nutty seed.

Greenhouse—Structure used for cultivating or protecting tender plants (or chicks).

Hardy—Ability to thrive under very cold or warm conditions. Toughened.

Hatching box—Small heated box that houses eggs very close to hatching.

Hatchling—Recently hatched animal.

Hide—Skin of an animal whether raw or tanned.

High metabolism—Rapid process by which an animal converts its food into usable energy.

Humidity—Amount of moisture in the air.

Huxley, Thomas Henry—English biologist (1825-1895.) He told other scientists that dinosaurs and birds were related.

Incubator—Large heated box where egg embryos develop before hatching.

Instinct—Ability to react to a situation without conscious thought.

Insulated—Separated from a source of heat or cold.

Lean—Muscle tissue that contains little or no body fat.

Livestock—Farm animals kept for use and profit.

Mulga and Sheoak—Heavy strong Australian hardwoods used for making boomerangs.

Nanotyrannus—Smaller adult relative of *Tyrannosaurus rex or* possibly a *T-rex* juvenile.

Nomads—People who roamed from place to place, usually with the seasons.

Ostrom, John Harold— U.S. paleontologist (1928-2005) who proved that birds evolved from meat-eating dinosaurs. He discovered *Deinonychus*.

Outback—Areas in the middle of Australia, far from cities and towns.

Oxygen—A colorless, tasteless, odorless gas that animals breath in or absorb.

Paleontologist—Scientist who studies the fossils of plants and animals.

Parasite—Plant or animal that lives on or in another plant or animal (called a host). The parasite receives all or part of its food from the host. Parasites are generally harmful to their hosts.

Petri dish—Small round glass or plastic dish with a loose-fitting cover that's used to grow bacteria and other microorganisms.

Pip—An internal pip occurs when the unborn chick pops its air sac. An external pip happens when the chick pierces its shell with its beak.

Pores— Tiny openings on the surface of a plant or animal that allow air or moisture to pass through.

Predator—Meat-eating animal that hunts and kills for food.

Preen—To groom or tidy, as when a bird puts its feathers in place with its bill.

Protein—Substance in meat, fish, poultry, cheese and some vegetables. It's essential for building and repairing tissues. It performs many other jobs that allow the body to perform at its peak. Protein also provides energy and stamina to prevent the body from tiring easily.

Ratites—Group of flightless birds including the ostrich, emu, cassowary, rhea and kiwi.

Reptiles— Cold-blooded animals such as snakes, lizards, alligators, crocodiles and some extinct dinosaurs.

Sinornithosaurus—Small 130-million-year old theropod fossil that showed primitive feathers on its body.

Specimen—A sample of material used for testing.

Spigot—Faucet

Stamina—Staying power, endurance.

Stance—A way of standing.

Sternum—Long flat bone located in the center of the chest. It connects with the ribs to form a "cage" around the chest.

Transitional—Passing from one stage to another.

Translucent—Transmitting and diffusing light so that objects beyond can't be seen clearly.

Theropod—Meat-eating dinosaur that ran fast on its hind legs and had short arms.

Tendons—Tough, cordlike tissues that connect muscles to bones.

Umbilical cord—Food supply pipeline that connects an unborn human baby with its mother.

Vegetarian—Animal that eats only fruits, vegetables, plants and nuts.

Vertebrates and *invertebrates*—Animals with and without backbones.

Veterinarians—Doctors who provide medical care and surgery for animals.

Warm-blooded—Having the ability to generate and maintain body heat.

READING FOR KIDS

Armentrout, David and Patricia Armentrout. Aug 1, 2008. *Animals That Fly and Birds That Can't.* Vero Beach, FL: Rourke Publishing

Bartlett, Anne. Nov 2001. *The Aboriginal People of Australia (First People).* Minneapolis, MN: Lerner Publications Company

Elwood, Ann. Aug. 1999. *Ostriches and Other Ratites.* Evanston: Zoobooks Series

_____ and John Bonnet Wexo. Sept. 2000. *Ostriches, Emus, Rheas & Cassowaries.* Evanston: Zoobooks Series

Fowler, Allan. 1998. *These Birds Can't Fly.* Danbury: Children's Press

Kalman, Bobbie. Oct. 1997. *Birds That Don't Fly.* New York: Crabtree Publishing Company

McGowen, Chris. June 2011. *Dinosaur Discovery: Everything You Need to Be a Paleontologist.* New York: Simon Schuster Children's Publishing

Mercer, Bobby. 2012. *The Flying Machine Book: Build and Launch 35 Rockets, Gliders, Helicopters, Boomerangs and More (Science in Motion).* Chicago, IL: Chicago Review Press, Incorporated

Murray, Julie. 2012. *Emus: Australian Animals.* Minneapolis: Abdo Publishing, Big Buddy Books

Silverman, Buffy. Feb. 2012. *Can You Tell an Ostrich from an Emu?* Minneapolis: Lerner Publishing Group

TEACHER RESOURCES

Books:

Flood, Josephine. April 1, 2007. *The Original Australians: Story of the Aboriginal Peoples.* Sydney: Allen & Unwin

Long, John and Schouton, Peter. 2008. *Feathered Dinosaurs*: *The Origin of Birds*. New York, NY. Oxford University Press

Lourandos, H. 1997. *Continent of Hunter-Gatherers: New Perspectives in Australian Prehistory.* Cambridge University Press

Lucas, Diane and Ken Searle. Feb, 2005. *Walking with the Seasons in Kakadu.* Sydney: Allen & Unwin

Ostrom, John H. 1984, *Dinosaurs*, ed. J.J. Head. Burlington, N.C. 27215: Scientific Publications Department, Carolina Biological Supply Company

Brochures:

Facts for the Teacher: About Emus- © The American Emu Association, updated 12/9/2011

Facts for the Teacher: Dromaius Novaehollandiae- © the American Emu Association. Updated 3/20/2010

I Suppose Your Wondering--What's an Emu?- © The American Emu Association updated 12/9/2011

Information and Organizational Materials:

American Emu Association, 1201 W. Main St. Suite 2, Ottawa, IL 61350. Phone: (541) 332-0675 or info@aea-emu.org

"The School Lesson Plan - Emus" is a new online resource for teachers. This informative overview of emus and the products they provide starts with a review of the Ratite family that includes ostrich, emu, cassowary, rhea and kiwi. This slide show guides the viewer through the many unique qualities of the emu. After the comparison of the members of the Ratite family, the slides move on to the emu skeleton, hatching emu chicks and the many products produced from this amazing creature. This totally usable bird provides nutritious lean* meat and moisturizing emu oil.

> CD of School Lesson Plan—Emu. Updated 6/16/2010 (cost $15.00 plus $5.00 shipping)

> To order, contact:
> *Emu Today and Tomorrow*
> 11950 W. Highland Ave.
> Blackwell, Oklahoma 74631
> Phone: 580-628-4607

S.T.E.P. Student Training and Education Program—Emu

The Emu Project Record Book is ideal for 4-H members, FFA members or anyone who has an emu and would like to keep a detailed record of their project. The record book was originally created as a part of the Texas Emu Association's Student Training & Education Program (S.T.E.P.). This program is no longer active but, the 37 page Emu Project Record Book is now available as a CD and can be ordered for $10.00 from *Emu Today and Tomorrow* and will soon be available as a PDF on this site.

> To order, contact:
> *Emu Today and Tomorrow*
> 11950 W. Highland Ave.
> Blackwell, Oklahoma 74631
> Phone: 580-628-4607

Please note: While there are many emu product suppliers listed on the web, the American Emu Association hopes that you will consider shopping with AEA's Certified Business Members. In order to be a Certified Business Member, suppliers must meet two rigid requirements by providing proof of liability insurance and sending in an analysis of their oil, proving that it meets standards set in the Emu Oil Trade Rules. www.aea-emu.org/wheretobuy

Hands-on Materials

Emu eggshells: Medium, large and extra large. All shells are blown, washed and sanitized with one ¼" hole. Visit our website's Products page and then click on the Eggs category. Phone: 855-608-8224 or leave a message through our website's Contact us page.

www.SugarMapleEmu.com

Double plumed feathers: Range from 1" to 18" long. You can choose from four sizes of emu feathers: small, medium, long and extra long. Toll Free: 888-383-9513.

www.uniquelyemu.com

Essay Contest

Contact http://www.redoakfarm.com/win_emu_feathers.htm for details

Songline Emu Farm:

66 French King Highway

Gill, MA 01354

413-863-2700

www.allaboutemu.com/songline-emu-farm

4-H Clubs

Contact Cooperative Extension Service in your state. Each state has an Extension Service office at its land grant university.

Or:

Go to: http://www.4-h.org/get-involved/find-4-h-clubs-camps-programs. Follow the prompts to find a 4-H office near you.

National FFA Organization
P.O. Box 68960 FFA Drive
Indianapolis, IN 46268-0960
Phone: 317-802-6060
Find a local chapter: https://www.ffa.org/about/localffa/pages/becomeamember.aspx#

BIBLIOGRAPHY

BOOKS

Jones, Philip. *Boomerang: Behind an Australian Icon*. Adelaide, South Australia: Wakefield Press, 2004.

Minnaar, Phillip and Maria. *The Emu Farmer's Handbook*. Groveton, TX: Induna Company, 1992.

Minnaar, Maria. *The Emu Farmer's Handbook, Volume II, Commercial farming methods for emus, ostriches and rheas*. Groveton, TX: Nyomi Publishing Company, 1998.

Lourandos, H. *Continent of Hunter-Gatherers: New Perspectives in Australian Prehistory*. New York, NY: Cambridge University Press, 1997

Ostrom, John H. *Dinosaurs*, ed. J.J. Head. Burlington, N.C. 27215: Scientific Publications Department, Carolina Biological Supply Company, 1984.

Sloan, Christopher. *Feathered Dinosaurs: The Origin of Birds*. Washington, D.C.: National Geographic Society, 2003.

PERIODICALS

American Museum of Natural History. "First Dinosaur Found With Its Body Covering Intact; Displays Primitive Feathers from Head to Tail." Press Release. April 25, 2001

Cracraft, J. *"Phylogeny and Evolution of Ratite Birds. " Ibis.* Vol. 116, Issue 4, pgs. 494-521. (1974)

Ostrom, John H. *"Archaeopteryx and the Origin of Birds".* Biological Journal of the Linnean Society. Vol.8, Issue 2, pgs. 91-18. (DOI: 10.1111/j.1095-\8312.1976.tb00244.x (1976)
_____. *"Archaeopteryx." Discovery*, Vol. 11, Num. 1, pgs. 15 to 23. (May 1975)
_____."*Archaeopteryx* and the Origin of Flight". *The Quarterly Review of Biology* 49 (1): 27–47. (Mar. 1974). http://dx.doi.org/10.1086%2f407902

Valde-Nowak, P.; A. Nadachowski, and M. Wolsan, "Upper Paleolithic Boomerang Made of a Mammoth Tusk in South Poland," *Nature, 329 (1987), 436-438*

Wong. Kate. "Dinosaur Discovery Shows Feathers Came before Flight." *Scientific American,* (April 26, 2001)

Yale University Office of Public Affairs. *"* In Memorium: Internationally Renowned Dinosaur Expert John H. Ostrom", (July 20, 2005)

UNPUBLISHED INTERVIEWS

Johnson, Stanley. (partner/owner Songline Emu Farm). Multiple interviews and conversations at farm in Gill, MA and by phone. September 2007- June 2008. Often during fall 2010, weekly during February and March 2011, periodically through summer and fall 2011 and into 2012

Kirkendall, Lara. Outreach Coordinator the Sacramento Zoological Society. Communications to identify source of information re: emu wings as body cooling system

Mares, Dee Dee. (partner/owner Songline Emu Farm Gill). Many interviews at farm in Gill, MA., by phone and email. Many trips to farm to observe and learn and photograph. September, 2007 through June 2012

Minnaar, Maria. (artist and co-author of the *Emu Farmer's Handbook* and the artist and author of the *Emu Farmer's Handbook*, Volumes II). Four email communications resulting in permission to use her illustrations in book. October and November 2011

Morgan, Armand. (Instructor at the Peabody Museum of Natural History, Yale University, New Haven, CT). Informational interview confirming dinosaur/bird connection. Viewed mold of *Archaeopteryx* fossil. July 23, 2008

Reavis, Joylene. (Emu farmer and Public Relations person, American Emu Association). 18 email conversations. October 2011 to May 2012

ELECTRONIC SOURCES

American Emu Association: "Eastern Equine Encephalitis (E.E.E.) Outbreak." http://www/aea-emu.org/node/582

American Emu Association: "Nutritional Comparison of Meats." http://www.aea-emu.org/node 36

Australian History: "Portuguese Explorers". http://www.australianhistory.org/portuguese

Commonwealth of Australia. The ScIslands. "Aboriginal Technology" © 2012 http://www.questacon.edu.au/indepth/clever/aboriginal_technology.html

Edwards, Ernest (1837-1903). Attribution for photograph of Thomas H. Huxley [public domain]. http://en.wikipedia.org/wiki/File:ThomasHenryHuxley.jpg

Emu Today and Tomorrow…your source for Livestock, Meat. Research, Nutrition, Leather, production. http://www.emutoday.com/

Geological Society of America, "Trotting with Emus to Walk with Dinosuars." 24 October 2006. http://www.geosociety.org/news/pr/06-51.htm

Georgetown University Dining Services, "Protein- What Does It Do?" http://www3.georgetown.edu/admin/auxiliarysrv/dining/nutrition/protein.html

Monroe, M. H. "Australia: The Land Where Time Began," A biography of the Australian Continent. Last updated 15/11/2008. http://austhrutime.com/aboriginal_history_in_australia.htm

New York State Department of Health, "Eastern Equine Encephalitis". www.health.ny.gov/diseases/communicable/eastern_equine_encephalitis/fact_sheet.htm. Last reviewed October 2011.

Regents of the University of California. "*Archaeopteryx*: An Early Bird"-© 1994-2006. http://www.ucmp.berkeley.edu/diapsids/birds/*Archaeopteryx*.html

Red Oak Farm. "Learning about Emu Feathers" © 1998-2012. http://www.redoakfarm.com/learning_about_feathers.htm

Schatz Publishing, Blackwell, OK 74631-6511. "Ratite Evolution: An Overview" *As seen in Emu Today and Tomorrow, Issue 1, Volume 7, January 1997* http://homesteademufarms.tripod.com/evolution.htm

Sacramento Zoological Society. "Emus: Dromiceius novaehollandiae" http://www.saczoo.org/Document.Doc?id=108

Texas Cooperative Extension, TheTexas A&M University System. "Emu Production." http://gallus.tamu.edu/library/extpublications/emuproduction.pdf

GRAPHICS CREDITS

INDEX

Alphabetical Index

Made in the USA
Monee, IL
14 October 2021

80002639R00064